the secret of you

Something to Whisper to Stars at Night

There is no secret you can tell that will
turn these pages away from you.

Somewhere on the other side of you, there is
a version of yourself that you know exists,
that perhaps you have been before, that you
remember at the edges of who you are.

This version of yourself is the kindest,
sweetest, most gentle version of yourself
who cares deeply about you and how you
treat yourself. But you try and lock them
away because that's what you were told to
do, or conditioned to do, or just do because
life has a way of slowly wearing you down
until you forget all about this secret
version of yourself hiding just under the
covers of who you tell the world you are.

This book is for the you inside of you. The
you others may have left behind.

(Whisper what hurts softly, and it will
slowly become every song.)

—pleasefindthis

the secret of you

poetry about shadows and light

iain s. thomas

Andrews McMeel
PUBLISHING®

Dear You,

I have not written

because I have been building silence around
everything I've ever said;

I am building giant fields of snow between
every letter and every word because—

in some secret way, just like you, I believe we
are entire universes, still expanding.

—Iain S. Thomas

I know if I'm going to do this again,
I have to be honest because that's all that's
left, and that's all this has ever been, a
race to honesty, a competition to see who
can be the most naked, where we show off
our scars, skinny-dipping in the moonlight,
and then are somehow transformed by the
words "I have that one, too, and that one,
and that one, and that one," and then, my
God, aren't we all beautiful?

I should write a list.

I should write about ████████████ how his eyes
kept staring at the top of the Christmas tree.

I should write about ███████████████████

I should write about how I can't explain why ███████
██
█████████████████████████ she says, "Everything here
is just so red, white, and blue."

I should write about leaving every part of myself
behind. I should write about the little things
people leave on the pavement for other people to pick
up: a punch bowl, a bookcase, a car seat, and the
little libraries, and the leaves overflowing, unbound
in the fall (that is what they call autumn here, and
it deserves a different word, because it is
different here). I should write about walking through
the neighborhood, trying not to seem like an idiot,
trying not to gawk, trying to say things in a way
people will understand—how do you put air in your
tires? Why would you build a house out of wood? Where
do all these boxes come from? I should write about ████
███████████████████ how scared she was because
she was worried that she was bad at hide-and-go-seek
██
██
██

I should write a list.

I should keep the score.

We should write down

the names of everything

and everyone

that keeps us whole,

that can never be blown away.

And then to speak

to who you

are

or

coul

be

I Do Not Fear Dying

What keeps me warm is the idea
that when we are born,
we are taken from the universe,
and when we die, we return to it.

And I believe I know what that feels like
—where you've come from
and where you will go.

It feels like the tiny space between your
bodies when you hug someone you love.

Whether that's a parent or a child,
or a sibling or a friend.
I think that feeling we feel when we do
that, when we hug, is the feeling of some
small part of us knowing another part of
it is near.

And I believe forever feels like what
happens when that tiny space between us
disappears.

(I think we can't know what death feels like, but because death is such a scary idea, we imagine that it's a terrible, scary feeling to be dead. But I think we can center the idea of death in a different place than fear. I think we can center it in the feeling of connection and what that feels like, because that's what death is: it's reconnecting fundamentally with the universe on a profound level, and what else does connection feel like? It feels like a hug. Or laughter. Or a late-night conversation that just won't end. What would a hug with someone you love feel like if it lasted forever? What would holding your child, or your parent's hand, feel like forever? What would laughing with friends feel like forever? I think when we experience these things, we are given a hint at what returning to the universe and reconnecting with everything and everyone that came before us might feel like.

I think we come back together in love, not fear.)

Too Late for Letters

Old friend,

I am not wishing you well
from where I am;

I am not writing
from my current address;

I am writing from the memory
we still share.

The Longest Walk to Me

I am not the person I once was

or the person I want to be;

I am just someone walking
toward themselves,

stumbling,

and carrying on.

A Small Truth of Quiet Things

Do not try to tell life

what it must be;

give your life the space it needs

to become what it must become.

A Word of Caution for Travelers

The greatest pain I've ever been in

was when I thought

there was somebody I needed to be,

because I didn't know

who I already was.

Terrible Rules for Terrible Times

Remember the rules for writing

about dead fathers or mothers:

It can't just be sad; there has to be

some kind of cleverness to it

that makes it seem like you've moved on,

or haven't, in some smart way.

But I am both just sad

and shit at following directions.

Where You Were

You are young,

and so you do not see

you are living in some
kind of future,

and I am old,

so I'm living in some
kind of past.

(Why would you rush?
Every day was given enough
hours, and if it's not done
by the time you're dead
—who's going to care?)

(Maybe retirement is not really just retirement, or we're using too soft a word for the desire to not die cold and alone on a street.)

In Good Faith

I did not talk to God for decades

until my son's body lay stiff, shaking in my hands,

his eyes off in the distance, seeing

perhaps

the other side of life,

and in those minutes, after the 911 call,

I bargained, darkly,

until the paramedics burst through the door

and a man, no older or younger than me, took him

from my arms,

held him to his chest, and said firmly,

as he moved with purpose and grace,

no louder or quieter than it needed to be,

a three-word prayer for all assembled

to follow him:

"Go. Go. Go."

Return Tickets

I have not been to Hell

but I have sat outside the emergency room

in my pajamas,

smoking, after I had quit smoking,

and there,

I have touched cold, white, eternal flames.

I have never seen water turned into wine,
or fed five thousand people,

or spoken to a burning bush,

but a woman has told me,

"He's getting oxygen.

He's going to be OK. It's OK."

And Only He Knows the Words

God sings a secret song

for everyone who's ever stood in the cold,

white fire of pathetic failure

and shame

and said,

"I will carry on."

(How do you turn pain back into love?

Show me so I can touch God's face.)

(How?

How?

How?

How?)

The Thing You Lose

I think you have to give something
up to become who you are.

I think to do something really big,
you have to give something big up,
because life takes space, and the
more space what you're doing takes,
the more it has to displace.

So when you see someone in the
public eye and everything they are
or have is perfect,
I figure they've got something big
at home, when the lights go out and
the cameras turn off, that they're
missing.

I promise I will wait for you in
Heaven.

On the Other Side

I want to do this properly,
but time and time again,
I just walk in and throw a
corpse on the table
and say,

"Here. This is the thing
that killed me."

And that is the poem.

In the Middle of Everything

Stuck between
my parents dying
and my children being born—

"What was he like?"

You would've loved him.

You would've loved her.

A Dark Side of the Earth

There is a side of the Earth you can look
at that has no land, and suddenly, the
world becomes alien, and the sheer amount
of water you're looking at just doesn't
make sense.

I believe every heart has this same side.

A Messenger, a Runner

Trying to hold the
electricity
of some old joke
I barely remember alive,
so I can make you laugh
like he made me laugh.

Trying to hold the feeling
of her fingers through my
hair
when I was sick
so I can make you feel safe
like she made me feel safe.

From a quiet white page

my love will return as a flame

and remind you that there is a good reason

why all paper burns.

A Harvest of Sorrow

Like loaves and fishes,

the real miracle is the

ability for a politician to

take one tragedy

and turn it into thousands.

The Brutally Mundane

-How would you explain number-line theory
to a seven-year-old?

-How long to travel to the sun
on a skateboard?

-Where is the nearest trampoline place?

-Write a song for a seven-year-old to sing
about how much they love their cats.

-How do I comfort a child
after an active-shooter drill?

The Final Day

If you must hurt each other, then
hurt each other, but do not hurt
children, or the weak, or the frail,
or the very old.

If you must hurt each other, then
hurt each other, but do not hurt those
who do not want to fight, whose only
sin is wanting a warm, safe room,
whose only sin is being born here, in
the place where you want to hurt each
other.

If you must hurt each other,
then hurt each other,
hurt each other,
hurt each other
until there is no one left to hurt
each other anymore,
and only children remain.

God,
come and
get your
children.

Every Single Day

Wake up,

watch the news,

have a little cry,

join the meeting link.

Watching Tonight's War

If anything was possible through sheer

force of will,

all children would be safe,

but they are not,

and so we know: Will is not enough.

A Sacred Plea for Hands

Jesus, if they want pain,

put your nails in their fathers' hands;

give them a way to hold their pain

instead of giving it to others.

The Falling of Dust

You are walking ash,

scattered with every step

whenever the wind of truth blows.

Time and Time Again

Here is war:

building the next ten thousand years of pain

from the children who survive

to tell their grandchildren one day

what their grandfather did,

so they can murder a son or daughter

somewhere, generations from now,

you'll never meet.

Here is war.

I Will Remember

I have had friends

who were all the food,

shelter, and warmth

I ever needed in the cold.

The Best of Me

Just trying to write this down before I forget—
"Dad, can you wipe my butt?"—
trying to figure out something for the other one
to eat—and it's not like I have the
difficult job—

and these are the good old days.

Cleaning up vomit out of car seats—
it mixes with beach sand, and sleepless in the
hospital, and, Jesus, what is he doing now—

and these are the good old days.

Firstly, why were you in that kind of store to
even begin with, and secondly, how did he
manage to pee on a rack, and how did the dog get
chewing gum in its hair—

and these, I swear I know, will be
the last things I miss one day.

(I think if you zoom real far back, and you ask
why we're here and what we're here to do, I think
we're here to experience love in every way we can.
I think that our universe and our experience of
it is one way of experiencing love, and I think
when we die we go somewhere else and engage with
this fundamental force within the universe from
a completely different perspective. I think we're
part of a cosmic heartbeat, a kind of equation that
must exist in powerful waves, and I think that
the space between the numbers is a roller coaster.
(Love is the firework that holds us closer and also
the name of something we cannot see, something we
can only define as the sense that we are connected
and yearning. I don't know what love means, but I
feel like I know what it is.))

The End of the Song

In black shadows dancing,
will they call your name
when it comes time to answer
at the end of every life:

Did you find each other?

Did you find each other this time?

Forgotten Bottles

You are

somewhere far away,

alone in all that you are,

and

I do not intend to bring you

comfort

when I tell you that I am alone

in all that I am

whenever I am not with you.

I tell you just to tell you.

(If there is anything that matters,

it is still underneath our fingernails

and in soft sand

and in water

and in salt

and in sunlight

and in feathers.)

Shimmering in the Dark

I had a dream
every word I wrote

grew wings

and flew away to find you.

To find you

A Warm Place to Mend

Have you ever made a list
of everyone you know who's died?

It's a room that starts off empty,
then haunted, and over time,
becomes something else entirely.

.

Telling Time the Truth

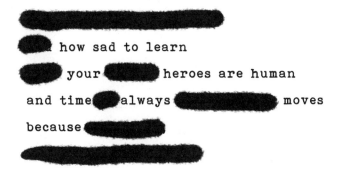

█████████████████████

██ how sad to learn

████ your ████ heroes are human

and time ████ always ████████ moves

because █████████

██████████████

██ now,

now just feels like something

waiting to be then.

(I'm sorry I haven't called;
it's so much easier to sink
into silence.

(To run your fingers across
another person's skin and
start a small fire in the
universe, in the space
where you love them.))

(Can I just say, to be moved through
time, so rudely and constantly—
it's too much.)

The Typography of Land

Every place holds a scar
you can only see
when you speak to a child
who grew up there.

a different time.

Endless

I don't know how to write without

it being a conversation with something nameless.

Every word these days

is just a prayer to what I've lost.

(I am trying to find the
words to describe the
silence that comes after
you leave the room.)

(I just want to be good
at being alive.)

To light up the shared constellation.

To be the story with no ending, together.

To change, and be changed.

In Quiet Praise of Forgetting

Let go.

Holding on causes pain and frustration.

It feels like a soft, beautiful poison that you both want and do not want at the same time.

So when I can remember and when I have the presence of mind, I let go.

I let go of anger, resentment, envy, even longing and nostalgia; however, those last two are the most difficult to let go of at all. But we must.

It doesn't mean we cannot visit things that used to make us happy, but we must remember that we cannot stay.

And Now Here You Are

When you were born,
you gave love
its new name.

(The world ends when someone gets fed up with traffic or they lose their job and all hope, or it ends when something so tragic and terrible happens that they just can't imagine carrying on. I think we each have our own world, and while we only ever see a version of the world played out in culture around us from a really big, high-up point of view, the way we experience the world is as individuals. So I think for millions of us, the world is ending all the time; it just doesn't make the nightly news.

It's also important to remember that people are hanging on just a little bit longer than they thought they could and discovering something new about themselves all the time. Someone is reaching out for an opportunity and discovering another hand reaching back to grab them. Someone is just taking a deep breath and deciding to try again tomorrow.

None of those things that are happening, and are always happening, make the nightly news either. And it's good to remember that.)

Maps of Strange Value

No tattoos.

Just maps to places
I buried my heart.

The Ballad of Home Improvement

You're crying in Target again.

You're lost between home improvement
and office supplies.

You forgot why you walked in, but
you're here, so you might as well find
something to cry about.

You thought too long about a song.
Or what home used to mean.
Or how someone looked at you once.

And now you're crying in Target again.

Not Quite Legion

When you're too many

people at once,

there's not much room

inside you for

yourself.

A Tiny List of Inconsequential Things
That Make Me Happy

The muscles you use

to hold someone close to you.

The train you're late for,

running late.

Someone Needs to Ask

You're working at a job

because the alternative is death,

and you've got to wonder how

advanced we are if that's life.

(And maybe if you're too honest,
your heart falls out.)

God's Own Truth

And all your best songs
are the ones you've never sung
because as long as you don't sing them,
they've got nothing to become.

(I'm still on the line,
waiting in case you pass out
so I can call someone—
and what's used you,
you should know:
it's used others too.)

Like Veins across a Country

It calls

and it calls and it calls

and I'm doing my best not to answer.

I Would've Said:

Just don't die.

Just hold on.

Just stay.

Simple Facts

Everything you can write about
silence:

Stop the Universe

I don't know how to begin again
like the silence in the space
between the fingers and
the strings of the guitar
I am just waiting
for something beautiful to happen

Forgotten Songs of Make-Believe

You can't tell me
the future isn't born in broken homes
outside small towns
in New Jersey
in not knowing what to put your cereal in
in anthems sung by starving kittens
in the lost
in an empty, dying mall
I'm trying to forgive
everything
in ██████████ blue eyes
I am trying to:
reach into the silence
and pull out God's voice

Still Whispering

I am holding in this feeling

in the fear that one day I won't,
and in the end, it will sound
like nothing at all,

just a sigh in an empty room.

(It's OK.

Put reverb on your wounds.)

The Essence of Now

Maybe hope is a

new notification,

as banal and sacred

as anything else.

Maybe all we are

is waiting

for something to break

the silence.

Just Trying

Trying to pull the white space

toward itself

until it becomes something more.

Trying not to mess up

whatever good things you've got left to give.

(One day you will wake up and
your first thought
will not be about all this.)

Something Defined by
Its Absence

We're never in love with our
moment, always just the
moment before,
when we think things were
better, or more real, or
something else that we can't
describe, just miss.

Across a Table

Maybe it's only been you

and me forever, sitting

across from each other, in

a thousand different ways.

Life takes a while to wear in,

sometimes

all of it.

Fragmentary Collapse

And maybe everyone has something
somewhere inside of them—you might
be good at a sport or an art that
hasn't even been invented yet, and
quite honestly, the most important
thing you can do is just look, just
check, and if you're not good at
anything, well, forget everyone and
just make up something new that only
you can do.

For the Love of Banshees

Screaming through
whatever's left of the real.

Spiral-bound notebooks,
spiraling.

The Starter Pistol

The squire hit my great-grandfather through the face
with a riding crop and the other one threw his dinner
plate at the wall and we've been running ever since,
every single one of us, from him to me, running from
the man who, by at least some accounts, was his father,
our father's father's father.

In Silver Shadows

"Tell me a secret," they say,

and I can't say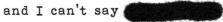

so I tell you something else,

and I lie,

and I keep every secret.

Wait:

I will write you down
in amber and hold you
up to the light.

This is the only way I
know how to love.

I'm sorry.

Unforgiven Light

You can pull down the fire of
everything and you've done it with
nothing and even if they took nothing
away from you—you could still drag it
from the stars in the sky, kicking and
screaming.

There is some
scarlet, spinning, shining jewel inside
of you and nothing,
nothing the world has ever thrown at
you has slowed it down.

Even when you sleep, it spins on.

Everything was good.

And it was strange to notice that,
and how rare everything being good truly is.

Character of Fire

They had a presence like a
magnet facing the wrong way.

(In the end, God keeps the
receipts, or at least that's
what I'm praying for. I want
to know, my bones need to
know, if I was right, if I
was the good one.)

Bad Mirror

You are sitting at a typewriter with no ribbon,
writing ghost words onto pages that don't
remember what was said or who said it,
writing your story as a secret that only the
silence knows, pushing on the reverse of the
letters into the fibers of dead trees, just the
physical echo of what you tried to say but
couldn't.

Why can't you just write about forests or
something?

Why can't you write bumper stickers?

(I tried, and everyone just put the bumper
stickers on their hearts and drove them into
the ground.)

people think it's strange

that I'm not here

Shame and Guilt

I am worried I'm an idiot,
so I've spent my whole life trying to
do smart things; a kind of
incredibly productive pettiness
of the heart drives me
to try and do just one more thing
proving things to people
who probably haven't thought about me
in years.

(You should know now, the only way to stop
feeling this is to stop feeling anything,
which means that the next morning
you feel everything so much more.)

(I'm sorry, I'm in constant
conversation with the
best and worst versions of myself.)

Soon, It Will Be Someone Else's Turn

I believe that there is only one of us,

just one soul,

and it goes through all of us,

it goes through all of our lives,

one by one,

it lives an entire life and then
it moves on—

and slowly it learns
everything there is to feel.

Compression Instructions

Breathe anger out like old air
because that's all it is.

Admissions of Guilt

Maybe someone once told you

that if you did not write, the

sun would not rise,

and so when you stay up all

night, making what you make,

and the sun rises, you take it

as a sign that you're saving

the world, but maybe you're

just trying to save yourself.

(Go on.

Write something that doesn't hurt
for a change.)

(Who's asking?

The one asking if you can breathe
because one day, maybe you will
forget.)

Nine Points to Prove

You will reach through the fire

to who you are on the other side.

Introvert Prayer

I didn't leave myself at home

inside myself

for nothing.

Further Instructions

When you're done,

put me out under dappled light

and watch the sun

burn up what remains.

A Strange Crossroads Meeting

And only in dreams,
stars put us back together.

Last Requests

If, on my last night, the
moon asked me to come back,
I would say yes.

I would make myself again,
in spite of everything.

(We will meet there

where two paths join again

in a way only you and I
will ever understand:

When you touch my hand,
you turn an hourglass on
its side.)

Notes on Forever

On the other side of now,
everything is waiting,
and here you are:

a universe walking.

Constellations of Light

If you just track the
sadness and not the joy
across the sky,
you do your stars
a disservice.

You owe it to yourself to
remember good things
in the moments when you
can.

In the Spirit of Survivors

Not everything has been written down—
the color of a shell, the way that
water feels between your fingers—
there are some things that only the
human heart will ever know.

The Great Game

We play a game now because I told them

some people believe in Heaven and

some people believe in nothing and

some people believe you come back as

different things—so I tell them:

I will come back as air

and they tell me they'll come

back as sighs—

I will come back as dust

and they'll come back as sneezes—

I'll come back as everything—

they tell me,

well then, we'll be everything too.

The Reckoning

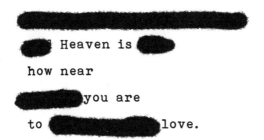

██████████████████

██ Heaven is ████

how near

███████ you are

to ██████████ love.

A List of Ingredients

Some people are made of
time and other people of
moments, moments things
changed, when people
came or people left—and
when they meet you,
they carry that with
them.

(The quiet in your heart

is singing.

When you listen, it grows

louder.)

Nothing Hurts in Dreams or Death

Late at night I try to make peace with
wherever my dead parents are and—
my father is driving his car forever
through the Lake District and the day
is crisp
and beautiful, no
my mother and him and all of us are
parked in a car looking out over the
sea
and we are eating hamburgers and
drinking milkshakes, no
my father isn't anywhere; he's in every
kind thing I do, every ounce of
kindness he showed me
repeated into infinity, no
my mother's in Heaven, no
she's feeding the birds in the garden
in her pajamas forever, not caring
ever what anyone thinks, no
she's in a wooden box, next to my
father's wooden box—where is the
appropriate place to keep your parents'
ashes?

A cupboard is too dark, a shelf that

you can see reminds you over and over,

they're dead, they're dead, they're dead,

no

my mother and my father are waves

reaching the shore, no

they're all around us, that's what I

tell the kids; they're always here as

long as we remember them, no

they're sleeping, no

we're all in my father's Triumph TR6

and he is well, and his legs work and

nothing hurts, no

no, no, no,

no, no,

no.

Fields of Phone Booths

In a place called Merstham in Surrey, they
keep all the old red telephone boxes on a
patch of land no more important than any
other.

At night, if you walk near them, you can
hear the sound of ghosts falling in love.

My Last Warning

My son,

I am going to count to three
and then march into God's house
and pick you up and carry you home.

A Good Reason to Start Anything

There was a pizza place in the town I
grew up in and now it's gone, and
every now and again, someone posts ███
████████████████████ saying that they
miss it.

Now I have a favorite burrito place
███ that ████ will be gone someday
soon too.

It took them two weeks to find
██████████████████ sooner than when
the universe will experience what
scientists call heat death.

What are you waiting for?

Eternal, Endless Ticking

Sports make a good clock for life—

the players: are they older or are they

younger than you are now?

Which actor have you chosen as the one
you'll watch get old and eventually
die with you?

In the Key of Eons

Forever stretches out, both behind and in
front of us, and in our brief,
maybe meaningless lives,
we are bridges to the infinite.

Amongst the Lost

And now nothing matters.
or has ever mattered.
or will ever matter again.
and even when everything ends, when
the sea boils off to show everything
that sleeps beneath, I will still be here.
and I will still miss you.

(You will never know what to be, and the greatest mistake you can make is thinking that you finally know, that you have reached the truth of who you are and you will never need to change again. We are so many, many things, and our brains desperately try to convince us that we're just one thing; we're just our job or our relationship, or we could be our hobby one day if we tried hard enough—and there's this tremendous sense of freedom attached to that idea, that we can give who and what we are a name, and when we do, we'll finally be free. But we won't. We will be one thing for a while, and then we will be another thing, and the vast, vast majority of our lives, we will be many things— and accepting that and making peace with that, letting go of the name you think you need, is where true freedom lives.)

A Snow-Covered Park

Fuck it.

There is always
time for forever.

(I think you never really settle and you have to
give yourself permission to change. I think that we
get so caught up in who we are and the things we think
we want that there's a good chance you're going to
wake up one day, look around, and realize that none
of the things that you worked for, that you swore
would finally make you happy, actually do make you
happy. And this terrifies us and fills us with
existential dread because if we're not who we think
we are, then who are we? And the truth is, we
aren't anyone. We're only ever becoming someone.
We're becoming the next person we need to meet on
this journey. The person we need to be to take the
next step. We're becoming more in touch, or more
refined, or developing our sense of taste, and a
million other things that just point toward this
idea that we're always going to be in a state of
flux. You don't wake up and despair that you're not
you; you wake up excited to meet the next person
you need to be.)

In Praise of Moments

And when our eyes, and our hands,
and the tips of our fingers.
And when our hearts, and our
bodies, and the smell of your skin.

And when, and when, and when, and when,
and when, and when, and when, and when,
and when, and when, and when, and when,
and when, and when, and when, and when,
and when, and when, and when, and when,
and when, and when, and when, and when,
and when, and when, and when, and when,
and when, and when, and when, and when,
and when, and when, and when, and when,
and when, and when, and when, and when,
and when, and when, and when, and when,
and when, and when, and when, and when,
and when, and when, and when, and when,
and when, and when, and when, and when,
and when, and when, and when, and when,

and when, and when, and when, and when,
and when, and when, and when, and when,
and when, and when, and when, and when,
and when, and when, and when, and when,
and when, and when, and when, and when,
and when, and when, and when, and when,
and when, and when, and when, and when,
and when, and when, and when, and when,
and when, and when, and when, and when,
and when, and when, and when, and when,
and when, and when, and when, and when,
and when, and when, and when, and when,
and when, and when, and when, and when,
and when, and when, and when, and when,
and when, and when, and when, and when,
and when, and when, and when, and when,
and when, and when, and when, and when,
and when, and when, and when, and when,
and when, and when, and when, and when,
and when, and when, and when, and when,
and when, and when, and when, and when,
and when, and when, and when, and when,
and when, and when, and when, and when,
and when, and when, and when, and when,
and when, and when, and when, and when,
and when, and when, and when, and when,
and when, and when, and when, and when,
and when, and when, and when, and when,
and when, and when, and when, and when,

Everything Is Temporary in Eternity

We are teenagers smoking cigarettes

in kind-of-stolen black cars,

trying to fix the jammed tape deck,

getting strangers to buy beer for us,

hiding in your mom's backyard—

we are young again,
staying up all night like—

it's nothing, finding songs
that mean forever,

even if we always knew
forever wasn't real.

A typewriter with no ribbon.

The Revival of Songs Passed

It's simple:

You give your fire

and you give your heart

and in the cold that remains

you must build yourself again.

A Dirty Mark

You try to scrub away the parts of

you that you do not like,

not knowing you are trying to

clean the dirt off a mirror.

In Secret Sight

In the dark, with the

lights out,

no one but you knows that

sometimes

your eyes don't close.

Tremors at the edges of what was.

Tremors at the edges of what still remains.

Shaking at the thought.

The Things You Do

You hold your tongue,

even though it carries your heart,

and your heart has become heavy.

(Treading air, desperate for
the place that birds go,
where summer still lives.)

In Dark Light

Never forget, when
you ask, "What if?"

—this is what you
wanted.

—this is what you
once begged for.

Hidden Still and Silent

They think you have a light

that only you can see,

but there is also a shadow

that only you can feel.

A World of Lines

Some of us live in a world made

entirely of tightropes, and so we

are slow, and careful,

aware that at any moment,

we could lose ourselves.

In Unquiet Rest

In softly blooming nights you lie

somewhere black oceans beckon,

the undertow pulls you down,

and with all your soul,

you pull back.

Who Would, Who Could

You're the pillar to all of them,

and yet late at night,

in the darkest of hours,

one must ask:

Who picks you up when you fall?

Who gives you what you need to feel OK?

Knowing What I Know Now

Wait—I know now,

our blood was born in the stars,

so when we're arguing,

it's not actually us;

it's just the universe colliding,

trying to figure itself out.

(Talk to me like it's the end of the
world and I still matter.)

A Maxim

All I know is how I feel,
and I wonder if you feel
as lost as I still do
in the middle of the night.

(When we see each other again,
all our conversations will start simply
with, "Do you remember when?"
and then we will laugh or cry
or both, or at least,
that is what happens
when I think about it happening.)

A Beautiful Machine

In a world built on bullshit,

let your heart be a machine of brutal truth.

The Fifth Season

Tell me what changed you—
and I will show you what changed me.

One day,
there will be a season of us,
and we can change together.

A Moment in the Silence

Wait; sit with what hurts.

Sit with what hurts and hear it.

Take the time you need to heal.

There is no good miracle

in turning pain into more pain—

I know it sounds

like I am asking you to be some kind of God,

but in truth, I am asking you not to be.

The Art of Being Me

On my darkest days,
I have survived by pretending
that I woke up and chose to be me—
not my problems or my challenges
or even my successes,
but I did choose to be me,
out of everyone else
I could've been this morning.

What if we're only in love because
we love emergencies?

Refrain from Doing This

Pay attention because this is good advice:
Don't give your happy to stupid.

Stupid will say it's special, that they'll treasure it
forever, then they'll forget it under the couch.

Don't give your happy to heartless, to careless, or to
waste of time.

They will suck up precious seconds, hours, and days of
your life that you could've spent dancing a dance that
only you know.

Don't give your happy to success.

Success is fleeting and goes as easily as it comes.
In fact, don't give your happy to one day,
or someday, or any day.

Your happy is worth more than any single 24-hour period,
no matter how close or far.

And for the love of God, never, ever give your happy to a
billboard; even if the billboard tells you
that it'll give it back to you with interest, it won't.

Billboards always lie. Especially about being happy.

Don't give your happy to memories, no matter how clear
they might feel; the greatest liar is always the past, and
even if you think the lie is a good lie, it'll have you
throwing your happy away and walking backward into
the sad.

Now you might think, if you keep your happy,
no one can ever take it from you. But holding on to your
happy forever is just as bad as never letting it go.

Your happy was meant to be given. It was meant to grow.
It was meant to travel. It was meant to discover distant
shores and it was meant to see the sights.

Your happy was meant to be loved and held by
someone else. So give your happy, but give it carefully
and thoughtfully.

Give your happy to simple things that cannot lie.
Give your happy to the things that only you can do.
Give it to making something, like a life, a child, or just
the sky on a clear day, on a walk, in the air.

Give your happy to something that challenges you.
Give it to the sunlight coming. Give your happy to a cat
or a dog.

Give your happy to the stars on a late night.

Give your happy to the infinite.

Give your happy to someone you trust to hold it and care for it and grow it and treat it with the respect it deserves.

Because the right person, thing, or experience will give your happy right back, with interest.

Just don't give it to stupid.

A Day Like Any Other

The best day of your life will drift right by you.
Your team may win, you might get a new car, and
maybe you'll be there when your son or daughter is
born, but those are just special days, not the best.

The best day of your life will feel just like any
other, but the leaves will be turning red, the food
will taste a little better, and for some unknown
reason, someone you love will hug you a little
longer—and you will smile as you fall asleep that
night and never think of it again.

Even if you say "you must remember this" under
your breath, you won't.

And that is what will make it everything.

the best day of your life.

A Way to Come Back

Look at your life;
become aware of the grain and texture—
because your life has brought you here,
and it is worth taking the simple, hidden
moments and using them to understand where
this moment, this one here, has come from.

This one.

This one.

This one.

A Song Unsung

A shitty day is no place
to bury the songs you
didn't sing.

Get up and scream.

Instructions II

Lose what's left of me when most of me's
gone—there's no use in crying over spilled
milk, and in the end, we are all,
both ourselves and the ones we leave behind,
just a big mess.

(In the end, the doctors will open us all up
and find nothing but the ashes from
burning pages.)

For the Love of Whispers

Here you are,

so close that talking

becomes a way of

breathing

together.

A Box of Magic Tricks

Show me how what I feel isn't real,
and in the air between us,
God himself
couldn't convince me
I couldn't reach out
and touch whatever this feeling is.

As Close as Damn

Oh, when you're there and they say,

"Hey, how do I know we all see the same colors?"

and you want to tell them

you're sure you see the same thing,

at least between the two of you.

Over the Edge

You're not here,
and the things you aren't saying
could fill every ocean.

A Movement in the Water

Everything seems steady

but the trembling and the shivering

of it all; oh Lord,

you are always

just beneath my skin.

Falling to Pieces

You lent a shoulder to cry on

and then an ear

and then everything

and now, seriously,

what's left of you?

The Insomniac's Lament

There is rest

and being in bed

and sleeping

and some other state

I find myself in.

A Constant Flaw

There you go again,

writing down what happened

in your pen without ink

on your pages without end.

(I believe there's a secret song
that only your voice can sing, and
if you sing long enough,
you find it.)

Even after you
I am still me.

What I Want the Poem to Do

In the poem,
I want to talk about how
blue the sky was
in the middle of the desert
and the forged documents on
the seat next to me
that would get me to my
mother's deathbed
through the pandemic road
blocks
and how quiet the car was
after I got the call that
she'd died
and how the audiobook
stopped
and how haunted every rest
stop and gas station was
along the way
and how every burger place
with a playground
was on the other side of Hell
with red striped tape across
every slide
and every empty ball pit
and I was the only one
asking for coffee
and something to eat

through a mist of hand
sanitzer.
In the poem,
I want to talk about what
albums I decided
to ruin
on the eight-hour drive home
knowing that whatever I
listened to
I would never be able to
listen to ever again
and how I had to come at
writing about this
from the side.

In the poem,
I float up with her
between the desert
and the blue sky
and the white clouds
and I get to hug her goodbye.

(I don't know how else to say this:

I come to you with a full heart, and all
I want to do is listen.)

A Limited Playlist

What song would you sing that didn't end
with the words

"What if I'm the fucked up one this time?"

Forgotten and Forgiven

And if you spent your whole life dancing,

I hope it was always more for you

than anyone else.

(Everyone acts like they know,
and I'm not sure I do.)

(Start from a place
of love.

Not good intentions.

Just love.)

To Be Forgiven

You're not stupid
You're not slow
You are not dumb
Your brain works
a little differently
It sees and hears so much
that isn't even there

(If I could go back,

I would tell you there is no
single moment of your life
that defeats you, because
there is something in you
that depends not on talent
or intelligence or strength
or any skill; it just burns
with the simple decision to
carry on.)

A Terrible Game

I want to be better than I am,
but I just end up being worse.

Somehow, this is your fault.

(Given enough time,
I can miss anything
and anyone.

Given enough time,
I miss you the most.)

For Prisms and Reflections

A picture is just frozen light,

and yet

when I look at pictures of you,

the light in my heart moves.

Things My Child Did that 19 Children in Texas Can't

From the bed, jumped on my back and held my neck too
tightly while laughing.

Got into trouble for being rude to her friend about
who would sit in what seat in the back of the car.

Argued with me about whether we would watch TV or
read bedtime stories.

Worried that she would not be able to stay quiet in
her Code Orange drill at school.

Told me she thinks dead people become stars.

So why not take whatever joy our
bodies can give us,
when our hearts and minds have
already taken so much?

Doing My Best

I have made promises to myself in the dark
that I cannot keep in the light:
I drink my words when the sun rises
and also when it sets.

(There is no story but your own and the
meaning you find in writing it each day.)

Sacrosanct

Washing the dishes has a sacredness in it
that you can see
just by accepting that all you're doing
and all you need to do for a minute
is the dishes.

To Be Remembered

In the middle of the candle flame,

the colors disappear,

and there,

if you listen,

every poem

ever written

lives.

I miss everyone you've been
since we last saw each other.

I miss whatever I felt
before I felt this way.

The Hymn of Lost Lovers

In this time
we are unable to be together
and so I need you to know:
I miss everything I have known
in your heart.
I miss everything that makes you,
you.

(The world would think us strange
to love and yet we did
so damn the world;
who are we if not strangers
to everything but each other
and love.
I do not care.
I love you in strangeness and
stillness.)

Everywhere on the planet I live in,

there are museums and memorials

to the moments we shared, and

every single one has a line outside.

Memorials to the
moments that
we share.

Let Go

Sometimes

the thing

you think

you need to hold on to

is just holding on to you.

(Who you are is not my fault.

Don't blame me for it.)

In Kind

If you promise me anything,
promise me you'll be kind to you,
be good to you, give yourself
more than enough,
be generous with your heart to you,
even when others aren't.
Especially when others aren't.

Give yourself the full benefit of you.

Not for Lack of Trying

No one will tell you—
you're meant to make mistakes
and people like to pretend
that they don't make them,
but they do, and that's OK.
It's all OK.

You have to be bad at something
before you can be good at it.

Forwards

Go
wherever your heart takes you,
because it is your heart, not mine,
even though you are in mine.
Even though you take mine with you.

In Truth

I can't tell you what it is,

but it is the reason

we are in this crazy experiment, with suns,

and gravity, and crickets, and fall,

and maybe

it's the feelings we share together.

To Feel Secure Once More

in Dark Places

What better words to end a story

than just

"And everyone was safe and home."

A Reminder of All That Could Be

And when I say you've got to hold on,

I mean to every good moment,

like a stone in your pocket
you can
always find.

Love, Dad

I can't wait for you to read;
I'm here and it doesn't matter
when you read this
or whether I'm alive or dead or anything

I'm here!

I'm here!

I'm here!

(I love you so much forever)

Not a Dirge But Close

Every day I am trying to sing

a song of goodbye

so nothing hurts

the way it hurt me

when the one singing my song

reached the end of their verses.

(Forever trying to stop myself
from making stupid decisions
that make it easier to make
more stupid decisions.)

We're all just scratching lottery tickets in the end.

The Stranger Turned to Me

I looked up from what I was doing

and saw you in the park and asked you

who you were waiting for

and you turned and as you turned

we found ourselves at our wedding

and I turned to you to say

"Wait, what—"

and you turned to me and we were in a house

with pictures of us on the walls and I turned to you

and you said

"Who are you?" and I said

"Who am I? Who are you and what's going on—"

and you turned to me and our children

ran past us and the girl held on to my legs, laughing

and you turned to me and

my back began to ache and I caught the reflection of
myself

in the mirror and my hair was starting to gray and I

turned to you and you had tears in your eyes

and you said, "Stop, please, stop," and I held your hand

and said, "I'm sorry, this isn't me, I'm not doing this—"
and you

turned to me at our boy's graduation and rested your
head

against my shoulder and said, "How is this happening?"
and I could not answer

but your head felt good against my shoulder, even if

it was my mother's funeral, and I

turned to you in the empty house while we waited for one
of them to call

and said, "If I had known, I never would have—" and you
turned to me

as I turned to you

as you turned to me in the hospital bed, holding my hand

holding your hand, you turned to me and I turned to you

and I bent my head down and kissed you

and kissed you

and kissed you

for what will always feel

like the first time

and I turned to you.

Also by Iain Thomas

the truth of you

poetry about love, life,
joy, and sadness

iain s. thomas
Bestselling author of *I Wrote This for You* and *Every Word You Cannot Say*

Available wherever books are sold.

Andrews McMeel Publishing
a division of Andrews McMeel Universal
1130 Walnut Street, Kansas City, Missouri 64106

www.andrewsmcmeel.com

24 25 26 27 28 TEN 10 9 8 7 6 5 4 3 2 1

ISBN: 978-1-5248-9379-8

Library of Congress Control Number: 2024935135

Editor: Melissa Zahorsky
Art Director/Designer: Brittany Lee
Production Editor: Brianna Westervelt
Production Manager: Chuck Harper

ATTENTION: SCHOOLS AND BUSINESSES
Andrews McMeel books are available at quantity discounts with bulk
purchase for educational, business, or sales promotional use. For information,
please e-mail the Andrews McMeel Publishing Special Sales Department:
sales@amuniversal.com.

Enjoy *The Secret of You* as an audiobook, wherever audiobooks are sold.